Porthole View

Porthole View

lynne potts

The National Poetry Review Press
Aptos, California

The National Poetry Review Press
(an imprint of DHP)
Post Office Box 2080, Aptos, California 95001-2080

Printed in the United States of America
Published in 2014 by The National Poetry Review Press

ISBN 978-1-935716-35-8

CONTENTS

Acknowledgments

Gull with Telephone Wire

She painted a boat on the flat of the harbor,

filled it with box-houses and set it afloat.

It was their ark for painting, they said.

At first they painted together, then he went past.

A gull will take to a telephone wire,

lose itself at sea, then find a stick for a nest.

She had come to the houseboat to paint.

Soon he was Noah; she, whatever is a wife.

Barge with Houses in Moonlight

Six rectangles bounce a barge on moonlit ripples
as if the white shadow could reverse melancholy
begun like a handle on a hairbrush to untangle
how to live from how to make something last—
time so swift, so abominably slow
like miles of sea grass on a beach never combed.

She let it be, but the barge floated on, mythically
chanting a domestic *anon* and *anon* to surfaces
that would thicken until she told herself again
to be sensible: behave, in light of what can't
be taken for granted or granted as something
free but haunted; hence unused. Say how
a tangled morning bounces a barge to canvas—
how later, it merely drifts.

Color Definitions

Ultramarine:

eyes of wrinkled old men staring
          the vast apocalyptic abyss of Heaven
while Chinese doves fly

on porcelain—three fishermen carrying bamboo
          poles crossing a bridge frozen
in white and lapis lazuli;

Italian Yellow:

earth heat in August, limestone church where
          young girls in flowered chintz dresses
press cheeks to marble columns reaching rafters,

a pigeon perched before fleeing to brilliant
          corn fields beyond;

Mars Violet:

hemoglobin of purple and red, retinas of vireos
          remote in forests where old women hang
lanterns at midnight to scare wolves,

children under an eclipsed moon reflecting

on smoke-glass bottles with potions
from stray planets.

Wild Mint

Water curtains blown to see-through like sand
pouring from a child's lifted pail—
all *whiles* waiting on beauty.

Where is it, you ask:

> starched apron with crocheted hem,
> fingers wiping dust off a clove spice bottle
> raincoat hood deferring first sprinkles

fact of being here six a.m. with shells, sea sparrows,
infinitude which, you have to say, is equal to mint-
pedal blue, early August.

Abstract on the other hand:

> curvatures, sharpened apexes, pinnacles
> implied compliment, concept of pintails,
> (but not their drifting white necks.)

It's the Twentieth Century way—
history on a thumbnail about to turn vervain
dressed in highway gray, see-through nylon fuchsia.

Porthole View

Lethargy seemed less when viewed from porthole level,
subliminal like that ring she wished otherwise
how wind made the mind turn liquid unsettled
like mackerel chine swilled to beaches,
stones marooned and couldn't think what to do
if she turned them over to paint—needing to frame,
ineptitude preventing her in rounds
like portholes or circles of lighthouse beacons.
Later in evening thinking *rescue* when someone sent
an alert signal—a trolling coast guard cutter lens
scanning the porthole (they called a scuttleside)
in case of flood—saving her from having to open
the hatch; she looked at the hinges of polished brass
her ten-cent ring worth nothing, in a way, everything.

Fragments from Letters
by Arthur Dove to Helen Torr

Dearest!
About 8 o'clock I discover I was in a bad way about being in love, if you know what I mean. You disappeared so suddenly.

*

Hope that porter got to you before you did all his work. The conductor said he would s—e—e—to it as he went by. Tell your mother not to let you carry anything.

*

Tried to fool myself last night with pillow and big fur robe. So come back and we will sew each other up for the winter in one bag. Hugs & kisses from here to Hartford for you. Ever

*

While waiting for breakfast fire to come up. Not such hot news about your not coming until next week. Am taking your book that Miss J. B. bought so you can read it before you come back "A Room of One's Own" by Virginia Woolf. I'm longing and want you to be here. Tons of love.

Delays and Contingencies

Some say *cabinet*, some *cupboard*: whichever holds

together best—

a few small modifiers between: dented silver tea

ball, shoe-polish tin,

open legs of a paper clip.

There's a way to decline an offer—shake or nod

in the opposite direction—

but what to do when you say to yourself:

throw it out or there's none left or give up.

Everything happened while she wasn't looking,

rather while she was looking at little reminiscent

things—coffee tin, broke shaker, glass bobble

on a window shade.

Meanwhile the buoy outside kept banging

the harbor sounding as if love could bear

all things, believe all things, endure all things—

even its absence.

Dove, Painting

Caught in a tree: it's a mind's-eye moon taking
a lifetime to acquire luminance without cheap tricks.
He had seen it backlit, cocked to one side
overburdened with boulders—too far away to tell
why it sagged but always it would, with gray paint
so he gave it another coat, then a thick rim
in pernod until whatever it had once been
turned to new, never imagined forms.
Whatever is nature stays under cover,
hidden like a stone's inside—freckled gray,
celadon, several tones of amber—all there
is, so he painted it. But what to do
when brush forgets stone, starts to paint
paint? He followed until he was lost in
stone – leaving everyone behind,
enfolded in its essence.

Foxglove

Past the sidewalk, branched path past the road bend
patched blue foxglove, beyond, skulk of fox grass,
ice-eyed blue lupine later pressed in a phone book
by her sister.

You have to handle her with kid gloves,
her father's aside to her mother.

Helen, oscillating between them
finally leaving her delicate white-button gloves
on the hall table—making the present
past in a train to New York.

Smell of Yeast Bread

Man came looking for work.
When I asked what kind—he said; I'm a parachute jumper.

Torr's diary entry

When he came to the farm that time urgent
he told her he wanted help;
she was in yarrow with a swap-shop basket
cutting stems with a pair of pinking shears.
Surprise he said, as if he had dropped the sky
she, the smell of yeast bread rising.
When she thought of it years later
it was mostly the yarrow she remembered.
Some thought it a cultivated flower.
She knew it to be wild.

Helen Torr and Arthur Dove: Part 1

Turn houses to squares, mountains to isosceles,
the eye a tricky aperture mincing light
and its attendants: crimson, azure, amber.
They would live on a yawl seven years,
bending for the low ceiling, heating with
wood and charcoal in the cast-iron stove.
How does one capture the soma of the sea?
Watch until transparency turns liquid topaz.

*

Look to the bottom of a coffee cup; sea
and house turned water. She was tea weary—
fainted pink, pale scent, trace of bitter.
Marry me a little, she had said, and it
happened. Outside the boat window
the storm had cleared; he painted it pale yellow,
a serrated knife for lightning. She put it in his
accumulating pile, not far from her few.

Fishing the Sound

Sea bass, cod, flounder, fluke, stripers, sprat—

she imagined a long invisible line stuck

in the mouth of transparent

swimmers, hazardous wash of light

descending to inarticulate dark,

 carp and bullhead feeding the bottom

old hooks hanging

from their rubbery lips

phalanged open with watery breath.

Telling: It Takes a Lisp to Say—

Hibiscus, pretty if you don't lose the laces of your
patent leather shoes (any jingle will do if the day
is uncovered, hasn't lost its grip).

Too long from April bloom of early narcissus
to October, its fingering asters pulling roots
of malingered heat; hyssop on roadsides until
dust turns November to field stubble, dry mud.

Strange, the lure of wild mixes: weeds and flowers
year after year of human tinkering—hybrids;
how to put things together was the question—
say, making bouquets of dahlias with daisies,
different size shades for a hothouse roof.

Would an aerial view of the Geneva farm show
hibiscus, salvaged patent shoes and guttered
downspout as one? Take how a flower stays
the same millennia after millennia then one day
wakes up, inexplicably altered.

Flotsam

Hearsay the sea, much amuck, tires in the flotsam,

Stamford wash-up, Bridgeport sewer dump;

wing-tipped shoes, syringes, empty cans of enamel

paint bobbing like dogs in heat;

Darien hairbrush, baking pan from New Rochelle

wine cork floated from Fairfield,

Norwalk ironing board, barnacles attached;

awful the way flotsam goes on without going,

everything diminished one way or another—

how the world floats it, sorts it, absorbs it;

the boggled way it all keeps coming back.

Yes

I moved aside

my eye a slit that

didn't open

paper maché-

masked to look good.

I'd seen Brooklyn's cemetery

un-comely; come here

with your basket I said

of flowers.

I am your spit of land

negligible

masked as forage

in a garden

of engraved stone.

Tomato Pincushion and Green Paper Stem

First, rain creeping the front steps, screens,

glimpsing sequins in highball glasses—

wrinkly-paper wind; soft-tissue knock

to the porch door—then more insistent

making rattled staccato like catbird calls;

then rain smacking pine boards, binging

wine glasses, soaking bleached chintz azaleas

on the wicker cushions; whipped-up rain

tossing magazine pages to the floor, banging

dead-pan windows.

Rain, then, in a furor bursting the living room

slapping the faces of lamps, picture frames,

kicking end tables, throwing a tomato pincushion,

tin box of pins to the floor, wind pulling hair

so screams fill the house a foot deep, furniture swept

to a frenzied vortex—no subsiding until after

midnight, whisky bottles drained, rain finally spent,

sofa sprawled, pants on the floor.

White as Suggestion Only

Pillowcase white, a kind of innuendo—visual,

mnemonic, like suggestive effects on water.

Would you sleep on one? If you wake, the world

rocking, is it boat, bed or gray pencil drawing?

You know *while* as two peaches on enamel-white

sills waiting to ripen; one could do better, you

think over and over; then someone comes to wake

the day you thought would lapse or not, not

what you could grasp either way—bed-morning

symptom, spread as a quilt stretched to a yawn,

you hoping to remain neutral though you know

you must get up, make coffee, set the toaster, listen

to the radio's morning weather. Instead, you mind

your own pillow's white business.

Once a Pocket Watch Holding

Seeing as opposed to *seizing*—a painterly problem
        the two different as lid to Harris tweed
or hammer to muskrats
        making paths through crabgrass;

seized—how you feel catching scents of bent-
        over hemlock branches
at a lakefront cottage where you caught frogs
        when you were eight
shush of the refrigerator door before your hand
        found the lemonade;

seeing more a matter of the eye—
        surface certainty as in, *there's snow*
on mountains or *I see what you mean but I wanted you*
        to say it;

the *seized* object loved, a gold pocket watch
        your grandfather opened
letting you touch his swollen blue veins

the *seen* object, a glass vase given as a thank you
        for serving on a committee where you
didn't really do anything

seized if it grabs you by the collar and pushes
        your head underwater until you can't
breathe and just when you think

you'll drown suddenly releases you
to the magnificent air.

Fragments from Letters
by Helen Torr to Arthur Dove

Dearest, it was good to know you had had a talk with Dr. Bernstein who certainly speaks much the same language we do, so necessary when difficult things are to be said, and I do know there is readjustment for us both

*

This seems to be a stupid thing for me to have done. Your flowers are so gay, even gorgeous now. It was a sweet thought.

*

I've been longing to write but felt it would increase desire in you to answer. So did the opposite thing to one I wished to do. [My doctor] says I'm a really different woman from the one he saw his first visit, but the modern technique is the go-slowly one evidently.

*

I am perfectly contented knowing you are performing so beautifully and don't want to return until I am even more different from the swaying lily or screen door when I left.

*

You are the person to be considered and Dr. Bernstein is the one to know what you want or "whom" and why!! I am in a complete state of minding my own affairs— charming if it could last forever. Must work on it. Moods, conditions, almost everything pertaining to us, change so fast during degrees of illnesses and degrees of convalescence, that there is no "constant" or absolute.

*

You certainly are the boss now. Make the most of it Darling.

Don't ever think you have to mention any thing you feel like doing for, as I say, I am in a bystander position at the moment, and as you say, and I can quite realize atmospheric things have changed considerably since the 3 weeks I've been here.

Don't Chew Your Fingers

Sound waves shuttling pebbles on the cove's
lip line

bristled WELCOME mat between shore ribbons
and porch steps.

Paint the wave's lip amethyst was her first thought
stretching

for an image to turn abstract. She was coming
down the stairs in bare toes

thinking the hour somehow transparent quartz
pebbles nudged each other

to get ahead or not get knocked about. She would
make beige,

crimped from a branch off the willow,
carry the day.

Don't chew your fingers, she said to herself.
Don't say too much.

Fog Horns

Fog rolling sibilants for the Sound's
drowned drifters

past watery ringlets turns to a concentric purple.

Whose eye closes on mauve motions? Whose iris
is salt white

in whereabouts of the moon's floating dark?

If you shrunk the moon, would it have less
volume,

Helen wonders while he paints, squinting
to make the scene smaller

which she could do, fog floating her
to oblivion.

Easter 1938

Art has absolutely no existence as veracity, as truth… As a drug it's very useful for a number of people, very sedative, but as religion, it's not even as good as a god.

Marcel Duchamp

Easter story made to make the world look plausible,

someone said, Helen and Arthur admiring a park

calliope for the sheer frolic of primitive April

no matter whether a god ascends or descends

in light of a new Easter hat, blue flowers

with yellow satin ribbon

considering the scene neither event nor advent—

no miracle, no magical being—just coruscating

space with luminosities even a god would admire:

Easter light, hidden eggs in Heckscher Park—

oval shapes perfect as a child's hand parting grass.

Georgia, Otherwise

O'Keefe wished people were more like trees
line from Helen Torr's diary

Here's how you fill a pail

if you live on a Halesite Harbor houseboat

in knots of not working, paint not setting.

September, 1929:

you painted a quince sideways

in a porcelain soap dish fluted to pie shape

but did it make a picture?

You were borne along lisping February, an ice

floe broke loose, your work dented like a pier's

metal bucket or jumbled hangers you think

you'd unscramble but you've turned tree.

But Georgia turned bird,

grew wings and flew away.

Shoals One Day

Vagrant in time to catch

silhouettes of mourning doves

as the tide comes in.

A dream will make a house—

then a house will take a turn

become a shell of itself

fragile as morning slid off

to become days, decades.

What becomes us

becomes us

as once a house where

we lay down

became as we will

one day shoals

and all the sea.

Walking Night Gowned

Feathered dust on the calendar with travel ads that
take her to a desert—thinking fragments of hallum
sedge blown to beige earth in an African village—
all she could conjure, pacing, gown wrinkled
like bunches of dry grass, last bits of sun;
a calendar's left-over page turned to September—
X's on what had passed into oblivion, white paint
underfoot, holding her gown, so she dreamed shadows
of faraway children drawing pictures in the dirt
with sticks numberless pages, African time.

She'd never known anyone who'd been there—
her thoughts hemmed in, calendar fastened—
pampean continent's sand blown along
a streambed of infinite days.

Five Stones in a Row

Become what? Put a cover over

the first stone for shelter;

unwholesome the second lucent blue;

rasp orange the third altered by being

too close;

a more opulent puce the fourth

(the one for fun),

but the last will not catch

in the net nor hide

what you meant.

Metal Card Rack and Steam

When the linden spoke she listened and when
the cloud spoke she spread her mouth—
wind seaming itself to white surfaces, recumbent
air gathering stones.

In tawny mood she was borne back, made fresh
as linens, brand-new nothings, folds of herself.
Was it cicadas that day, or the metal skeleton
holding faded postcards in the corner store
that made her remember?

She saw clouds turn amber, sky red-berry hard
like tines of a fork left on a porch table while
her mother pressed clouds of linen to steam,
hems rumpled to the floor, shells in a wood bowl,
her mouth set stone.

Sky-flecked Outdoor Shower

Easel-shadows stuttered about the room,
shapes coming to mind. What was it like?
Tall order to tell, roughed wind, shrouded view,
sequestered light, herself: gawky, agonal, standing
for nothing under the bucket shower in the sky-
flecked back yard.

Working, one got praise for using vermillion blue,
haberdashery green, shasta yellow which she
couldn't do, the long untended knot inside.
She tried to stick these in a wine bottle to paint:
bark, feather, or was it regret that wouldn't settle,
rattling white-washed porch slats that yanked
the hinges, floor paint that wouldn't stop flaking
like a skeletal fish she'd found, partial to remnants,
discards, castoffs she bought as thrift
but served her as penance.

Spells

Air, washed hung sheet

flapping otiose heat

gathered to a singed

glass thermometer,

spongy consistency

of floorboards to her bare feet—

Turner's mist

settling the skin.

Sit still and let arms

wrap fog around, she thought

and why she was

by herself

in spells.

Burned

Like coddled eggs begun slowly

forgotten on the stove until

pan water turns to film,

walls, sills, milk pitcher

becoming a crusted yellow,

tan, brackish brown

until they burst, yoke flecks

splattered to cupboards, sink

when she remembers, runs

from the porch to grab

the pan now burned black,

frantically scouring

the bottom 'til it's clean,

almost seeming improved

but weakened, next time

more easily broken.

Plan Never to Quarrel

Her fingers lifted the matchstick for

a split-blue second gas connection

but what held her hand from being wooed

was what she didn't know though he said

Don't worry she suffocated,

flame finally extinguished.

Color of Water, Inside

What was always leaden gray of February frozen
to skiff sides,

lock-jawed except for rattling masts, lethargic skies;

what was there but expanse of oxidized green
in May when seas

turn restive, stumbling against endangered shores,
lathered, graveled;

then August's cerise, sienna moss—rain sluggish,
slapping patterns

of cotton dresses on overworked clotheslines,
reels ground to rust.

October then, a madder-rose onslaught of jade water
until November,

curdled waves, rolled to froth along edges
of Halesite rocks.

Color of water depending on the observer—

but who was looking inside—kettled steam
on the windows

an abundance of silence flocking the galley.

Wave

Wave as water's disturbed sleep
as paper caught in a bicycle wheel
as desert sand where camels pass.
Wave as half notes on lined paper
as hair in whalebone combs
as wind-slapped circus tents.
Wave as odd behavior
instant-anger unchecked,
mood oscillations.
Wave as animal instinct
coming back to remind
how it will not go away
Wave as ruined concentration
as echo in cave ceilings
as a garden gate swinging closed.
Wave as coming and leaving
without traces on a sallow-green
evening with a tint of teal.

Helen, Circus Wagoning Herself
Out of the Picture

You wanted melon apricot to color a circus flag
for flying yourself—wagons, bunting, fluffed foliage;
also a distant hill for a statement of landscape,
white with zipper effect on the tent, upper left
 interrupting gray's horizontal bedspread;
canopies as portend of what happens even
on a circus day (red kisses inside the moving wagon)
with exuberant decoration you can't feel but
it's all you want so you gather yourself
to take the road home, rest, which you must
because you're ill again, the parachutist gone
in an amber-rust mood, failing to convolute
vague emotions into affection.

Potted Plant

Market heliotrope succulent, meaning sucking
the life of. Period. No children. If you carried
one,
would it bloom? Laburnum the other flower,
every part poison, even a swallowed drop left
in a milk-glass vase. Would she do one or the
other?

Here's how to paint a houseplant: shade it mud
to maroon leave the stem chartreuse and pot it.
Would a calibration of child-shadow make
an undulation, incantation for the small
unmentioned?

No one asked.
She was drifting to a vague purple laburnum,
absinthe green in a distinctly absent way.

Shadows

Slinky, curling around couches, climbing walls
with distorted fingers,

flattened heads hanging off the sides of city halls,
subway entrances,

draped over closet doors, coming to bed before
he does to disappear threadbare,

necessitating light, say, from a lighthouse
with Fresnel lens

or giant probe in the sky from the Midway
at the State Fair:

monsters dragging their tails across hillsides,
through river gullies,

over golf courses, market parking lots.

She stood in the slotted light between the kitchen
door and broom closet,

gray figure stretching empty arms across
the room, yard, pond

until you couldn't tell where anything ended.

Anti-philosophical

—Aesthetics is for artists what ornithology is for birds.

Barnett Newman

But about the birds:
herring gulls pestering mist over Huntington
egret lifting one delicate foot on a water square
to see beyond reflection.

Birds flagrantly ignore concepts
of color to arrive at their inner artist.

And about the artists:
each has a bird flying in his breast that could
any minute, turn outrageous orange
with piqued teal tail.

Painters have beaks as points they'd like
to make if they knew how to silence
their inner critics.

What Happened

Massive super-continent lasting fifty million years,
taking one hundred fifty thousand more to break apart
become Africa, North America, the Atlantic in between;

then a spine of mountains along America's eastern edge
lasting another two hundred million years until crumbling,
sliding to form the Atlantic's Continental Shelf.

Ice shapes land into odd formations for millions of years
more until it melts, leaving swales, bogs, lakes with wide
swaths of rocks, stones, lithic boulders.

Connecticut Lake fills with stone and gravel to make
an island, the Sound mixing fresh water with sea
in the shallows of this new strip of land.

Indian tribes come to Long Island, tenth century B.C.
staying for its fertile waters, rich soil and natural beauty.
Then the artists followed.

Swinging Screen Door

Virginia-marble pink or was it magenta? *Spectral,*
she'd said, though late evening she'd thought better
of the conundrum, scrim of what happened when
bugs bit the skin their abdomens swelling,
screen door lackadaisical, marigolds a radial yellow.

Once she slammed brushes to a soup can rusted
from little use, sure sign of a lapse, lost time
getting back her way of painting pink as white
with bit-lip blood mixed in, imitating him,
converting scenes to recalcitrant abstract,

fleck of oil to translucent trees disturbed
by her serendipity neglect to secure hinges
on the screen door, all side effects, all expressions
with changed meaning over time, lingering
mosquito sensation on the skin like some
dismissive remark.

But hadn't she tried dismissing, making herself
a screen behind which she tried to hide
and couldn't paint?

Scribble a picture on an ochre field, dry it
on a counter where metal spoons from
the flea market leave a puddle of rust, cut pieces
of rope fisherman throw overboard, drifting
to the yard, and bushes with mosquito netting

to keep red-wing blackbirds from picking
blackberries as a gesture of thinking: she was
over what she thought she wanted to do.

Storm Kneaded into Dream

Mangy monster butting rocks up hills,
immeasurable heaviness, boulders lopped
against Halesite's night ballast, yachts
in forest-black water, violent sky,
someone crying,

Why did you say that ...why did you ...
then a tanker, or was it a water tower
with miniature stairs you must climb
someone breathing lead wash over wooden
chairs—
neap or tidal one couldn't tell
wind swatting like old scoldings

Why did you do that ... why do you always...
as if climbing attic stairs to where one could
escape,
freighter breathing charcoal smoke
wool stuffing one's ear to quit hearing
or to forget.

Helen's Foxes

Fox pulled from a phantasmagoria of foxes trailing
        their insolent rust figments of fox barely
shaped.

Where in the litany of sorrow hides the one along
        the shore, stopped by blabbering stones,

another making faces in the forest reflected to a
scolding
        window holding her breath with angry
eyes;

one between herself and the fox on a needlepoint
pillow
        poised to avoid showing its wear.

Once a grinning fox she tried to stop kept coming
back
        like a minnow in muck.

What had made her face fox-mean in such a short
time,
        she wondered, her jaw rigid and clamped?

What had she to do with the fox crossing yard
trees,
        tongue muttering something snide?

A fox in the shore bushes has his own way of
grieving;
        but what of one's own green eyes?

Tennis Ball over Gramercy Grass,
Life Otherwise

If you lived hillside she wondered what direction
time would take.

Here it came from New York City down
the Sound to the sea

imagining she heard it from where she stood
on the bow:

> someone stirring batter with a whisk,

> manhole workmen on Avenue B

> ball over a fence to Gramercy grass.

Second-hand time she called it, feeling it

come from Manhattan down Long Island

to the ocean's swallow miles beyond.

No, hillside life would be restful, house leaned

on slopes given to elms and lindens.

Here, time caught on hatch handles

pretending to be still but rustling her:

churlish water, troubled Sound.

Helen Torr and Arthur Dove: Part 2

Last day before winter arrived covering
yard bushes with gauze: that was ritual.
A crab's scuttle was something else—
an instinct she knew well. Well, that's how
one learns to survive a shell: protect yourself,
repeat the motion until it's habit
slowly, slowly the outline becomes
apparent – covered feeling, never recovered.

*

When he couldn't recover from pneumonia,
she had carried tea trays, pallet, paint—
framed his work in the hallway with faint light.
Some days sea and air were the same color
though she no longer called them by name.
She had lived her work by another hand
and that had been that.

Acknowledgments

Thank you to the following for publishing poems
from this collection:

Denver Quarterly: "Night Gowned" and "Waves"

The National Poetry Review: "Gull with Telephone
Wire," "Helen Torr and Arthur Dove: Part 2,"
"Potted Plant," and "Smell of Yeast Bread"

New American Writing: "Flotsam"

Many thanks to my teachers: Richard Howard,
Lucie Brock-Broido, Mary Jo Bang, and Mary
Rueffle, and also to Nance Van Winkle and others
who read poems and made suggestions: Brian
Burt, Emily Callejas, Amy Clark, Michael Perrow,
Emmett Tracey, Jonathan Weinert, and Leslie
Williams. And always, to Gardiner Hartmann.

Also from The National Poetry Review Press

Lucktown by Bryan Penberthy

Bill's Formal Complaint by Dan Kaplan

Gilgamesh at the Bellagio by Karl Elder

Legend of the Recent Past by James Haug

Urchin to Follow by Dorine Jennette

The Kissing Party by Sarah E. Barber

Deepening Groove by Ravi Shankar

The City from Nome by James Grinwis

Fort Gorgeous by Angela Vogel

Able, Baker, Charlie by John Mann

The Wanted by Michael Tyrell

Loud Dreaming in a Quiet Room by Betsy Wheeler

Guest Host by Elizabeth Hughey

Manual for Extinction by Caroline Manring

Inappropriate Sleepover by Meg Johnson

Please visit our website for more information:

www.nationalpoetryreview.com

www.ingramcontent.com/pod-product-compliance
Lightning Source LLC
Chambersburg PA
CBHW021511090426
42739CB00007B/561